Miracles that Keep Me Going

Miracles that Keep Me Going

Poems by Charlie Brice

WordTech Editions

Published by WordTech Editions
P.O. Box 541106
Cincinnati, OH 45254-1106

ISBN: 9781625494405

Poetry Editor: Kevin Walzer
Business Editor: Lori Jareo

Visit us on the web at www.wordtechweb.com

Also by Charlie Brice:
 Flashcuts Out of Chaos
 Mnemosyne's Hand
 An Accident of Blood
 The Broad Grin of Eternity
 The Ventriloquist

Cover design: Jim Hutt
Cover art: Joyce Savre

For My Teachers: Robert Fanning, Maria Mazziotti Gillan,
Diane Kerr, Jack Ridl, and Richard Tillinghast

And in loving memory of
Jim Harrison and Thomas Lux

Table of Contents

Hot Poems to Go

I hope my poems form a crispy crust
of couplets, tercets, and quatrains
and possess the tangy liveliness

of tomato sauce laced with garlic,
with metaphors worthy of the most
smooth and tasty mozzarella cheese.

Could my iambs and trochees surprise
my readers like pepperoni and Italian
sausage shocks their tongues? Will my

anapests appeal to their palates in the way
that anchovies attract their appetites?
Will the chomp of onions remind them

of my line breaks, each stanza a new
slice of a poetic pizza pie? Will
my poem's meaning be as inviting

and familiar as the aroma that rises
from that steamy Sicilian dish? Could
my words warm a room like that?

I

Writer's Block

So new for me. Usually
I suffer from logorrhea,
not its nasty little cousin.

What a strange discipline
writing poetry is. You
create a good one

and then poof! You may
never write another. You
can't blame the weather

for your dry spell or
the pandemic for your
empty quiver—only

your skimpy imagination,
your failure to order
life's scree, find your

soul in a nearby riffle,
or appreciate the composition
of a neighbor's coursed ashlar.

Inside there's a stickle
about word choice,
punctuation, or whether

anyone would find your
work a tiny bit interesting.
All of which adds to your

hebetude until, desperate,
you consult the back flap
of your notebook where

you've listed words like
scree, riffle, ashlar,
stickle, and hebetude,

words you can throw into
a poem—literary lifejackets
that rescue stranded bards,

keeps them afloat, prevents
their drowning in self-
criticism and doubt.

Enlightenment

They say the only Zen you'll find
at the top of a mountain is
the Zen you brought with you.

They say you'll be enlightened when
you discover that your starting point
was your goal all along.

I think of the drunken guru that Allen
Ginsberg loved like a mother, Trungpa, who
made W.S. Merwin and his girlfriend strip
naked against their will at Naropa in 1975.

I think of Sogyal Rinpoche confronted
by a young woman with whom he'd had
illicit sex—how the Dali Lama, who stood
next to him, broke down and cried.

Oh, the unending spiritual labyrinths we invent
to avoid admitting that when it's over, it's over—
that death isn't a dark room or an endless sleep,
but the absence of dark, the abolition of sleep.

After forswearing his meditation practice,
Martin Buber realized that "all real living
is meeting," right now, with those around us.

Kurt Vonnegut wrote that, in this life,
"there is only one rule...God damn it,
you've got to be kind."

And an obscure poet, Charlie Brice, advises
that after you wring out your washcloth
of religion, hang it up with
all your other hang-ups.

Braxton

Two old ladies pass me
in a Portland rose garden.
The one says to the other,
"I told Braxton, I said,
'Braxton, God could have
made the world in black
and white, but he gave it color.'"
How could something so utterly
idiotic sound so dear?

There's old God, his floppy
artist's hat snug on his head,
his pencil-thin mustache riding
up and down, his pursed lips
squeezed to one side of his
mouth and then to another.
He stands in front of his easel
and gazes at the colorless orb
that inhabits his multi-dimensional
canvas. It's our world!

He moves back, to the left,
to the right, gets close,
shakes his head. There's
something missing. A palette
appears balanced on his left
hand. *I've got it! Color!* He
dabs his mighty brush into
a glob of blue and smears
it on our globe, then conjures
Beethoven's Ninth Symphony
and dances while he paints. He

goes nuts with the greens,
the yellows, the reds, every
hue at his command.

He thinks of Braxton,
his grandma and his
grandma's friend, and
the lovely rose garden
that I, a nonbeliever, frequent.
And he thinks, *That's good.*

Grocery List

I know I need Sweet'N Low,
  large amounts of which I pour
into my morning tea. Oh, the paroxysms
  this causes my health obsessed
friends. I'm poisoning myself, they claim.

I counter that my Sweet'N Low consumption
  is an act of Buddhist compassion. I have auto-
embalmed myself with artificial sweeteners.
  The mortician will take the night off when

my withered remains arrive. He'll go home
  to wife and kids, to meatloaf, mashed
potatoes, gravy, and a foamy brew because
  I will have done his job for him.
What else do I need from the store?

Here I ruminate on the voice
  Socrates heard in the Crito,
the voice that wouldn't allow him to
  lie his way out of his execution,
flee Athens, or save himself.

Do we have enough butter? We go through
  vats of butter as if they were
filled with...filled with...well, butter.
  What about Nietzsche's
will to power? He meant will

over one's self, not other people.
        It took his antisemitic sister to distort
his writings so the Nazis could use them.
        Do we have enough Diet Pepsi?
Sweet'N Low isn't enough, on its own,
        to immortalize my insides,

Diet Pepsi is an essential ingredient where
        auto-embalming is concerned.
For Sartre, Hell was other people. Why?
        Because he thought the gaze
of the other always objectified the subject,
        that love was nothing other

than one subject's attempt to rob
        another subject of his or her freedom.
I know we need eggs, milk, and hamburger,
        but I'm missing something—
Rye bread? Frozen chicken cordon bleu?

Pepperoncini? Yes, pepperoncini! I love
        it's crunchy spiciness as I
imbibe a ham and cheese sandwich.
        And what about the noumenon?

What did Kant mean by that? My friend
        Carlos tried to explain it to me once,
but he kept calling Kant, Kunt. When our
        kids were little and played on the
same soccer team, Carlos would yell to his son,

Fuckess! Fuckess! when he meant focus.

If we were to resume our philosophical discussion, would he tell me to fuckess on Kunt?

Don't forget the radishes. I just love radishes, and bacon and liver, what a luscious combo.

I must add bacon, radishes, and liver to my list.

Penis Envy

The little girl envied the penis because,
as Freud wrote, she thought she'd been
castrated. Freud's disciple, Karen Horney,[1]
debunked that myth by demonstrating that

Freud's theory of the little girl's castration
was identical to his theory of the little boy's
fantasy about what happened to the little girl.

Horney's truth did not set Freud free. He went
apoplectic. Some say his cigar fell out of his mouth
as he berated Horney for her apostacy, but then
sometimes a cigar is just a dick.

The only place I actually *saw* penis envy
was in the men's locker room at my gym
in Pittsburgh where the schlongs were on view

for all the asses to assess. Imagine my skin-cobwebs
while Dr. B, a senior analyst at the Pittsburgh Psycho-
analytic Institute, stood next to me, jay naked, and
obsessively flipped his scrotum with his hairy hand.

Slap! Slap! Slap! Its vocabulary was trochaic:
fleshy punches that punctuated his speech.
So, when I resigned from the Pittsburgh Institute,

gave up my faculty spot there, I sacrificed my
opportunity to otherwise enjoy Dr. B's company
with his slaphappy scrotum. Freud wrote that
psychoanalysis was the "impossible profession."

Had he had a premonition of analysts like Dr. B
thoughtlessly flicking their kerbangers with
impunity? Could that be why Freud sat outside

of the patient's view—so no one could see what
the analyst was flipping? Or had Freud discovered
an ancient, heretofore forgotten, Zen koan:
What is the sound of one scrotum flapping?

Full Body Exam

The beautiful Dr. Barbara Baxter swept into the exam room, her
    flaxen hair draped over her white doctor's coat.
She was as beautiful as I remembered from my first visit in which
    she recommended that I receive a "full body exam."
She asked if I had any Irish in me because, I thought, Irish skin
    incubates the big C. I regretfully admitted that I did have

Irish in me. She laughed and began her examination. She eased
    down the top of my paper gown while telling me, in her
sing-song voice that, after she took her boards in dermatology,
    the examiners played recorded bagpipe music.
"Are bagpipes Irish or Scottish?" she wondered, as I felt her hands
    move down to my shorts. "It upset some people to hear bagpipe

music after the exam," she purred, and peeled off my tighty-whities.
    She studied my business, if you know what I mean, and then,
as if asking me to pass the salt said, "Would you pick up your penis
    so I can look underneath it?" She wants me to turn it over?
I thought. Well, if she grabs my balls, it will flip itself over.
    Then she grabbed my balls with her

unspeakably soft hands and noted that they sported some purple moles, but
    "nothing to worry about." Frantic to prevent the inevitable, I said,
"Did you know that the English hated bagpipes so much they considered them
    weapons of war?" She smiled, "There's a mole on your thigh, next to
your scrotum," she said, while still cupping my jewels. "Here, look at it." I raised
    my head, beheld the beautiful Dr. Barbara Baxter holding my nugget pouch

in one hand, while pointing to the mole on my thigh with the other. "I see it,"
    I lied, and lowered my head. "Do they play bagpipes only at funerals?"
she asked, a sugary lilt to her voice. "Oh no," I gulped, trying to control
    my quivering voice, "they play them at weddings, at all occasions."

"Turn over on your tummy please," the beautiful Dr. Barbara Baxter said.
    I obeyed and felt her hands nudge down my skivvies again. "
You have a mole on each buttock," she said, gently replacing

my underpants. "It's nothing to worry about." Her fingers on my heinie
    caused my lips to tremble, my toes to twitch. Had there been
a power outage my body could have served as an emergency generator.
    After my exam, the beautiful Dr. Barbara Baxter gave me extra
samples of hand and body lotion. How precious these emollients were
    to me—especially now. As a token of undying gratitude,

I promised, as we parted, to send her a CD of bagpipe music.

Trepanning

I flunked my license exam in clinical psychology
        by four points—a respectable score
for the over forty crowd in California,
        but a flunk in Pennsylvania.
Foolish me, I'd studied the body of knowledge
        the test purported to examine
when I should have focused on learning how
        to take a modern multiple-choice test.

Some of the items were all incorrect. You
        had to learn how to choose
the least incorrect answer. Should I have
        used that strategy with my patients,
encourage the least incorrect way of dealing
        with their depressions and obsessions?
Remember, only use Ivory soap when you
        wash your hands 200 times a day.

I fell into a deep depression. My analyst,
        a lovely man who knew as much
about psychotropic medication as I did
        about astrophysics, put me on Tofranil,
an antiquated antidepressant from the sixties.
        Almost immediately an impenetrable
plaster wall appeared in my large intestine that
        required enough daily Metamucil to

blow me up like an irradiated tomato. Then,
        Mr. Happy donned a sombrero and took
the fast train south to Tijuana where he embarked
        on a protracted siesta. Try as I might, I
couldn't get in touch with him, if you know

what I mean. So clogged and cramped
on one side, limp as a bizkit on the other, I
        thought of trepanning, the ancient treatment

for depression. The Greek physician would
        take an iron stake and pound it into
the melancholic's head. If the patient
        survived, he was no longer depressed.
If he didn't...well, at least they tried. Hippocrates
        observed that patients' depressions often
disappeared at the mere mention of trepanning.

As usual, the Greeks had the right idea.
        I stopped the Tofranil and enrolled
in a course on how to take multiple choice
        exams. I learned how to pick the least
incorrect answer, avoided forever the chemical
        trepanning prescribed by my analyst,
and passed my license exam with flying vapors.

French For Reading

It was the requirement I most feared. We
had to pass a language competency exam
to progress into the Ph.D. program.

I chose French even though my past romance
with that language had been mostly unrequited.
I managed to squeeze out a B in a brutal summer

course at the University of Denver so I could graduate
and then, at Christmas, 1976, I was beset with lingo
Franko again. This time it was French For Reading.

I found myself fifty-four chapters behind as we
entered Christmas break. Fifty-four chapters!
I also had to study for an exam in Heidegger's

philosophy which didn't improve my *Sein* or *Zeit*.
If, as Marty proclaimed, death is our ownmost
possibility, I hoped it would arrive soon.

       Fifty-four chapters behind!

How to catch up? I selected the Chatham College library
because it was close to home and I'd never seen any
of those rich girls congregating around the stacks.

I arose every morning at seven, ate a quick breakfast,
packed a sandwich and a thermos of hot tea and
drove to the library where I *parlez vous*ed Français

and read *Being and Time* for eight hours a day,
every day, during that precious Christmas break.
My sweet wife was justly *irritée, mais que*

pourrais-je faire? She wasn't anywhere near
as *irritée* as the security guard at Chatham whom
I called from the empty library one evening

after I'd lost myself in the ecstasy of always
already being *Da* in the world and hadn't noticed
the library going dark. I tried the main door,

but it was chain-locked from the front. The frown
of the buxom security guard, the creak of her leather
belt, and the roll of her eyes conveyed that

she was dealing with someone who had fallen
fifty-four chapters behind in his French class.
Freed from the tomb of tomes I passed my

French comps and my Heidegger exam and
reveled for the next nine years in the *être*
et le néant of my Ph.D. program.

Anniversary[2]

Billy Collins' poem, "Anniversary,"
tells of a baby being born on the day
someone dies such that the baby's birthday
is always a commemoration of the dead
person's life. Who died on my birthday,
June 7, 1950? I'm gonna crank up the
Google machine right now and check that out.

The only famous person I can find who died
on my birthday is Charles S. Howard, the millionaire
owner of the famous racehorse, Seabiscuit.

Oh for god's sake! How humiliating.
Who has heard of Charles S. Howard?
He's not famous, his horse is. Couldn't have
some internationally known novelist or poet
have died on my birthday? A Nobel Laureate,
or even a famous acrobat or lion tamer, or possibly
an all-around world champion bronco rider?

What about a guy who, single handedly, pulled
twenty fellow marines out of quicksand in Korea
after one of his hands had been blown off
so that he had, quite literally, saved them single
handedly? But no, the guy with whom I celebrate
every birthday never did anything but own a horse.

Who the hell was Charles S. Howard anyway? I bet
he'd never ridden a horse. I bet he spent his time
drinking mint juleps, smoking stinky cigars, and

reading the newspaper at his exclusive men's club
while he sat in a red leather chair that made fart
noises every time he changed position.

Then again, who am I to whine that no one famous
died on my birthday? What will the person born
on my death day think about me?

Oh great, on the day I was born some obscure,
unknown, minor poet, not even a footnote
on Duotrope, some verbigerator obsessed with
nuns and death who, as an atheist, claimed
he had no soul and whose soul, therefore,
had nowhere to go, died on the day I was born.
Not only didn't he own a famous racehorse,
he didn't even possess a famous moose,
or turtle, or anteater.

I want to apologize now, before my demise,
to the poor bloke or lass who draws my death
to commemorate on his or her birthday.
I'm sorry. Make a wish. Blow out the candles.
Live a good and decent life.

Unabomber Shoes

I hate getting dressed in the morning—
the monotony of stretching the tighty-whities,
socks, and then the shirt I've been growing
over my body for a week, the black jeans
I secretly worry are the only pants that fit;
finally, the shoes, the black New Balance
for my wide feet that my darling son calls
my Unabomber shoes.

He had so many delightful names
for our vulnerabilities: he called the boney
protuberances of his mother's comely feet
her "man toes." He called the thinning clump
of hair near my forehead my "Elvis Presley Patch,"

and once, when he was three and his mother was
wracked with pain from Crohn's Disease, he said,
"Let's throw the I-don't-feel-good in the garbage can"—
so poetic, but now the name Unabomber makes tying
the goddamned things at least a little interesting. Maybe

he sensed what my whacked-out Jungian friends call
"the shadow," the side of me that would love
to send a few special people a bomb in a shoebox.
Fortunately, I'm a techninny and would
most certainly blow myself up in the process
of cramming the dynamite, or C-4, or whatever
into the New Balance shoebox.

Just to be clear: while I find getting dressed
morning in, morning out, a mind-numbing
exercise in meaninglessness, the kind
of absurdity that could drive Sartre
to poison his own *hommelette*,
I vastly prefer being clothed to running
around naked. I'm sure the rest
of the world appreciates that.

Night of the Iguana

On the bathroom floor, can't move my left side.
I think it's my left side. Maybe it's someone else's
left side and my left side is fine.

The party's rockin'. I was rockin' —
five or six vodkas and Diet Sprite (have
to watch my diabetes), a few joints.

I was writing a poem in my head.
       Far from the abyss, it went, *I stand...*

I'll just get up and...I can't. Goddam, it *is* my left side.
Did I mess myself? I can't move to...
I can't feel anything down there.

Help! Help me! Please. Help!
There's no words. I can't get anything out.
I'll have to wait. Someone will notice I'm gone.
Someone will have to piss. I'll wait.

What's that scraping? What...Jesus Christ, it's a shrunken dinosaur.
It looks like someone boiled its face. A fuckin' iguana!
Who has a fuckin' iguana in their bathtub?

I must have broken a towel rack when I fell.
He's using it as a bridge. His way out.

How did the rest of the poem go?
Far from the abyss I stand...
something about *leafmeal*,
something about *the brindled plain*.

Oh god, I'm the poet in the play, the old man who
searches for an ending to his poem, for the genteel
southern words that will bring peace,
and when he gets there he...

That ugly monster is coming toward me.
They say that once they bite, they don't let go—
even when you cut the fuckers in half.

Far from the abyss I stand...

Elephant Loaf

For Jake Veurink

One humid afternoon my little friend Jake,
ensconced in his parents' red pickup truck,
stopped me on my walk up Townsend Road.
We got to talking about the circus. I told him
of the time Judy, Ari, and I watched
The Shriners' Circus in Pittsburgh.

At some point elephants entered the arena,
front feet on the bottoms of those ahead —
a marvelous march, a pachyderm parade.
Suddenly, they broke apart, began to dance,
twirled their huge bodies in graceful ogees
across the arena floor.

While twirling in the air, his rear end
facing the circus stands, one twirler let go.
Huge elephant doodoos as big as loaves
of bread, poop-projectiles, shot into
the stands with marvelous accuracy,
caused panic and hysteria as mothers
and fathers, boys and girls, who only
minutes before peacefully munched

on popcorn, peanuts, and hot dogs,
screamed and scrambled to get out
of range of those flying mud cakes,
but to no avail. As if they were smart-
turds the military developed to use against
our enemies, those fecal missiles plunged

into the stands with merciless exactitude.
Oh, the collateral damage when an elephant
loaf splattered into the seats sending mothers
and fathers to the rafters and causing little boys
and girls to toss their Cracker Jack boxes into
the air, their popcorn exploding at the heavens.
Splat! The caca-bombs kept coming! Splat! Splat!

And the smell? The smell can only be described
as the aroma generated when an over stimulated
Africana Elephantidea, fresh from his dinner
trough, engages in a bonafide fudge-a-thon
during a circus performance.

Oh, the joy, the glee, the belly laughs
this tale brought to my little friend Jake,
and even, if I may say so, to his good-natured
parents who, that day, and many others after,
had to listen to this story repeated over and
over again at their son's request and to
my unending delight.

The Truth About Alaskan Air

With thanks to James Brown,
Michael Dickman, and Ryan Walsh

you're a sex machine

a brand-new bag

the hardest working man in the breathing industry

every time you flex a muscle an earth quakes

jet across the stage on one foot
        it's a breeze

salmon air
halibut air
grisly air
deer breath

you will spawn

you'll feel good like you knew you would

igloos make you hot

no need for air conditioning or Xanax

your will to power   a war on your will

please please please please
(please please) baby don't go

40

II

I Don't Bother Much with God[3]

And she doesn't have much to do with me. I think
        she got disgusted when I decided that
humping my high school sweetheart in my basement
        was more redemptive than the tasteless wafer
a hungover Father McCormic placed on my tongue
        at Sunday Mass.

How embarrassed she must have been when she realized
        that Monsignor Harman was getting off
when he wanted to know exactly how I committed those
        nocturnal sins of impiety—code words
for masturbation—which ended forever my voluntary
        enclosure in confessionals.

The only time I believe in a god is when something so horrible
        happens that only a supreme being could be behind it. Think
the massacre at Sandy Hook, think the automatic fire at the country
        and western concert in Las Vegas, or my wife's constant,
unrelenting pain, especially my wife's constant, unrelenting pain—
        pain that treats her as an ardent sinner when her life has been
filled with compassion for others and care for our world.

Well, to be honest, I lied. I don't believe in a god even when the worst
        happens. Perhaps I should have lived in Ancient Greece.
I could have believed in Zeus. Now there was a god: married to his sister,
        Hera, and henpecked worse by her than Ralph was by Alice. When
Zeus got mad, he let go a thunderbolt and had done with it. When he
        wanted to fool around, he became a swan or a bull—even,
on one occasion, a cuckoo to get the girl to fall for him. Clearly,
        he was my kind of god: a god who identified as a cuckoo.

Switching Lanes

On that clear Thanksgiving Day
        our old van changed lanes
smooth as a red-tailed hawk
        rides thermals. I was headed towards
my brother-in-law's home in D.C.
        where turkey, dressing, sweet-potatoes,
and suspended resentments
        awaited our arrival.

Safely ensconced in the middle lane
        of I-95, sure that I was headed
in the right direction, I began to think
        of my parents' friend Barry,
the night he reached into my pajamas
        and fondled my penis
while I slept with him during his visit
        to our home in 1955
when I was five years old.

I'd asked if I could sleep with him
        in the way I might sleep
with a favorite toy or pet. That night
        he shoved his hand into my pajamas
and whispered, "Betty." When I told my mother,
        she laughed. "He must have
been missing his wife," she chortled,
        and laughed some more.

All those years I'd associated that memory only
        with my mother's laughter. But
on that pristine fall day, when
        our old van switched lanes
like an eagle swoops down and
        carries away a salmon,
I understood.

Taphonomy

The insects feed
Upon your flesh
And beetles burrow inside your chest.
                    American Folksong — Origin Unknown

Maggots magically appeared on the chicken breast
        I'd squirreled away in my Roy Rogers lunch pail
and stashed on our backyard patio. Cold Cheyenne nights
        didn't stop those grubs from their relentless gnaw.
My second lesson in rot.

My premier lesson involved the first time I tasted black rye bread
        (maybe 1955) in Cheyenne. Where had my mother
found such an ethnic wonder? In her kitchen there were
        two spices: salt and pepper. The most exotic
item at the butcher's was salt pork. That magnificent
        black bread tasted like nothing I'd eaten before.

So I stole a piece and hid it amongst my mother's underwear
        in her bedside table. A few weeks later, I remembered —
dug through some panties until I found the decrepit slice,
        parts of which had turned green while other parts had
little white plants springing from the crust.

Did this discovery stimulate a curiosity that resulted
        in my becoming a scientist who created life
saving drugs beyond antibiotics, or make me into
        a world famous taphonomist? Did this first
exposure to nature's detritus lead to precociously
        profound ponderings on the inevitability of death,
perpetual change, finitude, and temporariness?

Well...no. I couldn't stomach chicken for a year, and got
            in trouble when my mother found the moldy
bread which, in disgust, I'd stuck in between her
            cotton panties and a girdle.

My big takeaway?
            My realization why god,
in her infinite wisdom,
            created refrigerators
and garbage cans.

Silent Night

Dinah and Aaron's son, a Mormon bishop,
didn't allow them to attend his wedding because
they smoked and drank. Even though they tithed,
they weren't allowed inside the huge temple
in Salt Lake City where their son married
an upright Mormon woman.

All those years growing up in Cheyenne
I never met their son or daughter-in-law.
I'm sure this was because Dinah and Aaron
were shunned by them. Maybe that's why
they loved coming over every Christmas
to drink with my parents and spend time with me.

Every Christmas my parents placed an array
of gifts under the tree for me, their only child.
I'd open the gifts and find battery powered
trucks, cars, airplanes, games, and gadgets,
but my parents never bought batteries.
Those toys would fester on our living room
carpet only to disappear weeks later
into a lonely crate in the basement.

After a few years, when Aaron arrived
his pockets bulged with batteries. He'd get
my toys up and running in no time. One year,
when I was ten, I found a pair of skis under
the tree. Aaron showed me how to put
them on, took me out to our back yard
and gave me tips on how to ski.

Dinah had a big loving laugh. I remember
the lipstick stain on her cocktail glass
and on the filter of her cigarette,
the bright red polish on her fingernails
and how the sweet smell of bourbon
mixed with her lilac perfume.

By the end of those Christmas evenings
the four of them were drunk. My mother
would tear into my father for drinking up
the profits of their restaurant supply business.
Dinah and Aaron always scurried away.

Once home I bet they had a nightcap,
shared a cigarette, talked about how much
they missed their son, how huge swaths of
winter white packed Cheyenne's windblown
streets, and how there were no footprints—
animal or human.

Attention

Attention, attention must be finally paid
to such a person.

Arthur Miller

A lit Kent with its Micronite filter simmered
    between two sausage fingers of his right hand.
When he slithered the fag onto its resting place
    in the ashtray, that hand bothered a bourbon
and water. His left hand draped in surrender
    over the captain's chair at the kitchen table.
His left eye drooped—always a sign.

Were these his Guadalcanal days stretched
    into forever? Days of palm trees crashing
to earth, crushing his buddies in their tents,
    of monkeys hurling coconuts from tree tops
with uncanny accuracy at the sweat-soaked
    heads of GIs? His days in the evacuation corps
where, after bagging what was left of his comrades,
    he made sure the right dog tags accompanied
them on their last trip home.

"Do you drink like that, smoke like that,
    because of what you saw? All the death?"

Far away from me, although he hadn't moved, he smiled.

"What's up Charlesy?" He sipped his highball.
    "I can see that you're shaving now.
Don't let the razor drift too far up your cheekbones.
    You don't want hair growing up there."

Requiescat in Pace

My cousin Frankie was visiting with his straightlaced,
super-Catholic, draconian, disciplinarian, pipe smoking,
Hitler-mustached, father and his brainless, perfumed,
rosary-thumbing, cigarette smoking, bourbon drinking mother.

Frankie's dad was Mr. Neon in Seward, Illinois. By gosh,
he was successful, moneyed, and merciless: the reaper
of justice meted out to daily mass attendees and titanic tithers.
Somehow, Frank and I wound up on Pershing Avenue

walking/jabbering about Mickey Mantle and that terrific
Yankee team when we came across a dead dog. At eight-
years-old I had no idea what breed it was, neither did
ten-year-old Frankie but, as good Catholic boys, what

we knew and felt was that the crushed canine deserved a
proper Catholic burial like the one provided to Frankie's
Uncle Terry who, a drunken causality of Korea,
drove off the road to his death near Torrington

the year before. So, Frankie grabbed the departed's
front paws and I gripped his back paws and we began
the half-mile procession to my backyard under
a July blaze in ole' Cheyenne. When we got the

deceased to our destination, we were shocked at
the absolute repulsion displayed by our parents,
especially by Mr. Neon Super-Catholic whom
we expected would have at least admired our devotion

to the rituals of the one true apostolic faith. Instead,
my mother immediately immersed me into the most
secular of baptismal fonts—our upstairs bathtub.
I assumed that the same fate had befallen my cousin

Frankie, but when allowed into our basement, where
Frankie and his parents were billeted, I discovered that
a different denouement had been in store for Frank. He'd
been ordered to find a branch in our backyard that

could serve as a switch. I glimpsed him, briefly,
standing in his underwear with welts, bloody and raw,
across his thighs, flogged by his father, as Pilate
had flogged Jesus—and twice as holy.

The Fly in the Ointment

There's nothing like chasing that ball,
and even though I was a fat little kid,
so fat I couldn't squeeze under the gate
that guarded the softball field in Lions Park
but had to climb over the top and drop,

bounced blubber, on the ground—
even though I was a pudgy player, when
Gary hit that magnificent fly ball, I chased
that orb, timed my jump perfectly, and
caught it two inches over the fence.

Robbed as he was, Gary dropped his bat
and came after me. Gary was older
and even fatter than me. I outran him—
circled the outfield, then the bases,
until he tired. I still hear the smack in

my glove and feel the sphere's weight
in my left hand, smell that Rawlings
leather—the aroma of summer.
The next summer, when I was twelve,
Frank Hanken, our own Charlie Hustle,

the scrappiest ballplayer in our neighborhood,
did the dirty in the home team dugout
with Cherie, or Jeanie, or Kathy—I can't
remember. I do recall they were both
chewing gum when they dropped under

the dugout benches and have always
wondered whether they spit it out
or chewed on Mr. Wrigley during
their entire double play? Frank's homer
that day was a game-changer, a career-ender.

We never snuck into that field again.

The Old Days

Missile silos ringed Cheyenne—
enough firepower that, when we practiced
an air raid drill, the goal was to get home
before our little town became a gleaming
ion-field. Stars punched through the night
sky where I looked for big and little dippers
and the streamer that would end us all.

When Dr. Shwin visited he warmed his stethoscope
in the palm of his hands. Still, the frigid Cheyenne winter
left its signature on my chest. My father carried my stiff
body with its swollen ankles off to Memorial Hospital
where I spent six months of my fifth year of life
with a "possible" case of rheumatic fever, and where
radium-filled winds of Los Alamos and elsewhere
coursed through my bed-bound body—caused my white
count to soar. It took two bone marrow tests
to conclude that leukemia wasn't lurking.

Home from the hospital I heard stories around
the dinner table about wars, car crashes, and uncle
Johnny who spoke in a brogue, kept a mistress,
took daily communion, and fell asleep mid-sentence—
long before we'd ever heard of narcolepsy.

Grandpa wrote letters detailing his generosity
to a stranded family during a blizzard in Elco, Nebraska,
played piano (self-taught) for hours, instructed me on
how to smoke an El Producto, and "hiked" a mile
every day. Gramps changed clothes once a year

at Christmas. Mother burned the suit he'd arrived in
while he napped—replaced it with a suit from my
father, who had died from bourbon and despair.

Silo duty was a drag. The young airmen
that staffed those holocaust chambers,
guys who had, within their reach, the end
of the world, were bored and often drunk
at their posts. One night the drummer
for a local band was pulled off the stage by
MPs from Frances E. Warren Air Force Base.
He was supposed to be on silo duty
but went AWOL to play the gig.
That's how I got my job as drummer
for the Kansas City Soul Association,
the soul band that made my time
in Cheyenne, circled as it was by cataclysm,
a gift that could calm calamity whether
febrile, leukemic, or nuclear.

Hotboxing

We'd jam into the boys' room on the first floor at St. Mary's High.
Twenty squirming adolescents in a space made for eight or nine.
We should have renamed that bathroom the cancer ward. With
visibility near zero, the smoke-cloud so thick you could cut it
with a crucifix, someone would light a fag and pass the gleaming
death stick around. The idea was to keep puffing, one boy
to the next, until the gasper turned into a red-ashed lung dart
of unsmokeable heat and finally gave out. We must have smelled,
all of us, like the bottom of an ashtray left to bake in the back of a bar.

The priests and the few male teachers had their own restroom
and rarely ventured into our smoke-cave. Every now and then,
with no predictable frequency, Sister Hendrick, whom we lovingly
called "The Great White Whale" for her girth and pristine
Dominican habit, would open our bathroom door, gag and yell,
"You asses, get out here!" That's what we loved about her, the only
nun we had who swore. Still, we ignored her entreaties to exit our
pack-generated gas chamber, so obsessed we were, as Ahab with
his fish, determined to feed our addiction to capitalism's leafy Lethy.

Holy Smoke

It's a ghost but, like Casper, not scary,
not the kind that makes strange noises
in the night or seeks revenge on its murderers.

This ghost was not only holy, but one
of the Big Three: Father, Son, and Holy Ghost.
I think of the deceased Black Panther,

Eldridge Cleaver, inventor of Jesus Jeans,
who compared the Holy Trinity
to three in one oil, but I digress.

What did it look like, this holy ghost?
Because it was a ghost, it didn't have
a bodily incarnation. No images abound

except for the famous tongues of fire
that appeared over the heads of the apostles
during the first Pentecost. Tongues of fire—

fitting for a ghost to take the form that is no form,
the protean blaze that made Heraclitus think that
the only sure thing was change. Again, I digress.

When the nuns told us about the tongues of fire
descending upon the heads of the apostles, I,
of course, thought of the Sterno my mother

sold at her restaurant supply business: little
cans of napalm to light on fire and place
under stainless steel serving trays to keep

food warm on a buffet or to cook with during
a power outage. To me, this gift of celestial
flame insured that an apostle would never go

without a warm meal unless he needed to grab
something quick and cold, like a Hillel sandwich,
on the way to his martyrdom. Yet again, I digress.

Cowbell

I was in my teens before I realized that a cowbell originally dangled
from the neck of an actual cow. Did I finally encounter a cow
with its mini-gong swaying under its rawhide neck, or did
I see one in a John Wayne or Gabby Haze movie, or on one
of the ubiquitous cowboy TV series of childhood:
Roy Rogers, Sky King, Gene Autry?

Before my enlightenment a cowbell was, to me, the obnoxious tinny rattle
that some athlete's mother brought to one of our football games
and shook whenever our quarterback, Mike Barrett, hit Ace Evans
with one of his infrequently completed bombs during the perpetual
losing seasons endured by the St. Mary's Gaels in Cheyenne.

I put cowbells in the same category as other irritating noisemakers like those
straw horns that made awful noises as they unraveled when you blew through
them at some miscreant's birthday party or that goofy thing you'd spin
that sounded like a ratchet.

A cowbell came mounted on my first gold spackled cheap Japanese
drum kit. There wasn't much of a place for the cowbell in sixties rock
but I played it on *You Can't Do That* by The Beatles and *Honkey Talk
Woman* by the Stones—never connecting it with anything but
an outdated prop that added rhythm to a song.

I was a callow city boy far removed from the truth of what gave me milk,
what trod on the dust of dairy farms, and the white health squirted into pails
eventually transformed into cream and butter.

We are held hostage by our upbringing and the lacunae it inevitably creates.
A cowbell clanged of dung, dun, and dirty callused hands—what high school
football, asphalt, and amplifiers took for granted and left behind.

Coin Collection

I had a collection of nickels, dimes, and quarters
neatly tucked into slots on those green pages.
I remember Indian head nickels and Mercury dimes.

I was never ardent, never obsessed enough—couldn't
get excited about that kind of change. The change
that rocked me was produced by four lads from Liverpool:

I Want to Hold Your Hand, Please Please Me, She Loves You.
Their forty-fives cost fifty cents apiece. My coin collection
was gone before you could twist or shout.

Fifty years later, when my mother's mind set off
for nowhere land, I flew back to Cheyenne to spring
her from the booby hatch, close-up my childhood home,

and arrange her affairs, so I could get back to Pittsburgh
with her in tow—another day in the life. At the American
National Bank where mother had a safety deposit box,

I almost collapsed carrying it to a table. It was filled with
bags of coins, hundreds of dollars of pennies, dimes, quarters
and silver dollars—all circulated into total worthlessness.

Nothing in that drawer was real, but there was nothing
to get hung about. With a little help from my wife I got
Mother to Pittsburgh and into a comfortable assisted

living facility where golden slumbers filled her eyes,
where she ended the wild and windy night
of her long and winding road.

Dyslexia

Suzi's long straight hair,
the color of heather,
draped over soft
seductive shoulders,
her 14-year-old body
snug in the shift tightly
wrapped around her;

she introduced me to
Dylan's folksy drone.
We listened to Bob's wild
laughter during his 115th dream,
imagined him in the basement
needing eleven dollar bills
when he only had ten.

Suzi was cool, fab, gear!
My brain almost bled
while I obsessed on what
I'd write to her on the back
of my tiny photo from our
sophomore yearbook.

How to capture, in a
pithy phrase, not only
my erotic yearnings,
but the respect I had
for her intellect, the
silent dignity of her...

I couldn't finish. My
adolescent vocabulary
failed. My pounding heart
pummeled my resolve.
Overwhelmed by impulse
I quickly scribbled, *Suzi,*
you are such a sweat girl,
and handed my photo to her.

I watched her flaxen hair
jerk and quiver, listened
to her snap her tongue
against her teeth, the *tsk*
of death. *I'm such a sweat*
girl? she said incredulously.

I watched her walk away,
down the locker laden
hallway of our high school
and wondered why,
in God's name, I could
never learn to spell.

Haircut

For Bob Waliki and Jason Irwin

On the floor of the Frontier
Barbershop his cigarette ashes
mixed with his customers' hair.

Hank's right eye in a permanent squint
from the fog of the fag that dangled
from the right corner of his mouth.

His nose, brindled with busted blood
vessels, resembled a cauliflower
ear more than a proboscis.

He'd cut my hair since I was
a little kid, but now I was
thirteen and wanted to be hip.

Had I seen the "surfer cut" in the
pages of Life Magazine or in a
beach movie with Frankie Avalon

and Annette Funicello ? Oh how I
ached to see what was under
her Mickie Mouse tee-shirt.

I subscribed to Surfer Magazine.
Photos of dudes shooting down
a pipeline, hanging ten, dancing

on waves in Maui, Huntington Beach,
Rincon, and Santa Cruz papered
the walls of my basement in landlocked

Cheyenne where the only body of water
was Sloane's Lake in Lion's Park—
hardly big enough for a motorboat.

Okay, I couldn't surf in Wyoming,
but I could try to look like a surfer
couldn't I? Hank stood in front of me,

holding his clippers, flicking ashes
from his white barber's smock.
What can I do for you? he asked.

I showed him a photo of a guy with
a surfer cut: long bangs in front,
shorn close on the sides and back.

Uh ha, Hank said and patted the
barber chair for me to occupy
while he performed his magic.

There was the familiar buzzing
and clipping and the wonderful
fragrance whipped up in Hank's

shaving mug, the stropping of
the straight razor, the shaving
cream spread on my mug by

Hank's huge shaving brush and
the glorious warmth of the hot
towel on my head and neck.

How's that? he asked, and handed
me the mirror. He'd given me
the same flat-top crew cut

he'd given me since I was six years old.
He laughed when I handed him
the $1.50 for making me look, again,

like a no-neck monster. I walked two miles
home with no hat to cover the fact that
I wouldn't be catching any waves soon

or that Frankie's hold on Annette's
affections had been safeguarded by Hank
at the Frontier Barbershop in Cheyenne.

The Girl from Ipanema, Washakie Center,
the University of Wyoming, 1969

After Diane DeCillis[4]

Sunday dinner at Washakie Center was a washout.
        We had a rule: if you can't differentiate the meat
from the cheese or the spinach they dished out,
        Don't Eat It! UW was an agricultural school, a haven
for the semi-literate progeny of Wyoming ranchers who,

in between beer chugging contests and squiring wads of snuff
        against their lower lips and incisors, learned modern
techniques of breeding cattle, but who secretly believed that
        "animal husbandry" was the study of freaky relations
between a cowpoke and what he poked. The so-called "steaks"

served at the Washakie Center to us dorm-bound undergrads
        brindled with iridescence reminiscent of industrial
spill-bubbles or the necks of grackles. Clearly those noxious slabs
        were the result of insemination experiments gone awry.
As we watched waitresses, yes waitresses, carry platters of inch

and a half thick USDA prime into the private dining room of UW's
        football and basketball teams, we leered at our thin slices
of mystery meat and imagined steers collapsing, one by one, after
        white-coated gentlemen injected them with the foggy effluvia
of their looney laboratory ludicrousies. We feared that those

experimental errata landed on our plates! While enduring such
         anxiety-laden repasts, we were forced to listen to an unending
loop of Muzak that featured The Girl from Ipanema every seventh track.
         Naturally we associated this gorgeous piece with the culinary
catastrophe cast upon us every Sunday. It took years for me

to appreciate Gilberto's slightly off-key lilt, the brilliant backing
         of Mr. Cool's smokey sax, and the sacred mesh of their
sexy call and response—years to cast off the sense that
         The Girl from Ipanema comprised the soundtrack of
an agricultural conundrum of cosmic proportions.

Out of the Closet

Clothed in my cheap JCPenney's suit, holding a bible, sitting on a container
        of disinfectant that smells like murder, like what they'd use to clean
the war machine of the United States of America, sitting in the
        utility closet the president of my draft board called their "waiting room,"

the door ajar, I see Ben Ramone in his Sunday best. Ben who years before
        struck me out with his ferocious curveball during our Little League
All Star Game pleads with the board: Who would care
        for his wife, for his kids, should he be killed? They treat Ben
the way all Mexicans are treated in Cheyenne in the sixties. They are so
        discriminated against they aren't mentioned
in discussions of racial prejudice.

When it's my turn, I emerge from the closet with my bible and my convictions.
        I'm filing for conscientious objection in a state so conservative
it might as well be in the deep south. I tell the board that I'm a pantheist,
        make Spinoza's argument that all of nature is sacred, is God,
that to kill a human being is to kill a part of God. The old men on the board
        look perplexed—one falls asleep. A more sentient member wants to know
why I wouldn't kill for my country. "No people die," I quote Yevtushenko,
        "only worlds die in them." Who am I to extinguish a world?

Why not volunteer as a medic, another draft board don asks. I would, I say,
        but I'd treat the most wounded person and if that was a Viet Cong,
I'd treat him. One board member, an army colonel, turns white (or whiter).
        He must be imagining what it would be like to go into combat
with the likes of me.

Six months later, with trembling hands, I open a letter from my draft board.
        They have granted my request. I will never have to kill someone
I don't know, because someone else I don't know tells me to. But what about Ben,
        his wife, his kids? To whom did they hand the flag that draped his coffin?

Late Lament

Covered in the shroud of youth, I watched
so many funny, fine, and profound men
die from drink. I didn't let it sadden me.

I got angry instead.

Bob who used to say he wouldn't let
his female doctor touch his pierogies,
Carlos who called me his compadre,

Eugene whose last signature
on a consent form resembled
grapevine engravings on tombstones,

Mr. Jones who refused to eat,
would only drink milk, produced
the most foul-smelling pure protein poops,

or Jack, the former prizefighter and
champion drinker whom we all loved
and who, when asked to name the president

during his mental status examination,
confabulated that he couldn't keep up
with everything in the hospital:

They don't give me newspapers in here, he said.

I tested their poop, gathered their spit,
measured and emptied their urine,
massaged their feet and backs,

transported their bones and blood,
reverently deposited their wastes
down the conveyances of the

hospital industrial complex, bundled
them lovingly, put them on gurneys,
and took them to the morgue.

Today, fifty years later,
I cry for these men who broke
my heart over and over

when I was nineteen and had
just begun to inflate my lungs
with the breath of hope.

The Cremains Tour

I put my mother in the trunk,
her ashes tidy and cool in the UPS
box shipped from the funeral home.

My friend Jim flew from San Francisco
to Pittsburgh so he could drive with me
and those sooty flakes in the boot, back

to ole' Cheyenne where my mother had lived
for sixty years. Jim knew my mother, knew
that she not only didn't like me, but had no

idea who I was. He knew that it took a year
for my mother to comprehend that I was
a philosophy, not a business major, in college.

He knew about her outrageous temper,
her periodic "blow-ups," and her capricious,
string-attached kindness. But Jim didn't

know about the night she beat on my father's
chest, called him a drunken sot, a worthless
son-of-a-bitch, until his eyes rolled into the

back of his head and he fell backwards
into his favorite green recliner, the one
from which he loved to watch and laugh

at Phil Silvers, Red Skelton, and Sid Cesar.
We had to call an ambulance. Jim didn't know
that when we returned from the hospital,

my father in bed with oxygen cannulas up his nose,
my mother made me climb into her bed while
she wailed and swore to god she'd never say

another nasty word to my father. Jim didn't
know that, at nine years old, all I could do
was hold my breath and try to push her

meaty arm off my chest, the arm that trapped
me, in that bed, in that room, with her pink vanity
strewn with makeup and enveloped by the stale

odor of Chanel No 5. He hadn't seen how
she hovered over me, on top of me, while
making her brutal pledge, her huge fishy

carpmouth puckering my face with its
suffocating spirit-killing breath. He never
heard that high-pitched hissing sound,

as if a toilet had been flushed or a bomb
was zooming toward earth. Jim hadn't
seen or felt any of this, but he sensed it,

and drove my car with friendship deeper
than blood or bone. It took three days to
get her ashes to the Cathedral in Cheyenne

where the priest said all the prayers, helped
by an altar boy, really a man, whose muddy
sneakers beneath his white cassock epitomized,

for me, the history of the church I'd left
so many years ago, but to which my mother,
a white pall over the brown UPS box of her

ashes, remained faithful to the end. When
my turn came, I read for her the lovely song
from my favorite Shakespeare play, Cymbeline:

"Fear no more the heat of the sun," I, her only son,
chanted from the sacred pulpit while I wondered
for whom I intoned those soothing words.

III

Failing Up

My friend, Gus, carried the book *Failing Up*
        around like it was the bible
which, in a way, it was for him.
        Gus failed up like our cats threw up:
they couldn't learn not to lick
        wads of fur off their soft bodies,
so they puked—often and arrogantly.

Gus squeaked by with an odd job here,
        an even odder job there. Still,
he attracted a lovely woman who spent
        hours toning her body at the gym—
the gym where Gus would do a few push-ups,
        some casual sit-ups, maybe a knee bend
before retiring to the snack bar
        for a veggie burger and power shake.

No one was allowed to attend the wedding ceremony.
        Gus said it was too sacred to pollute with witnesses,
although their affenpinscher, Acne, stood up for them
        (when offered a biscuit), and a justice
of the so-called peace presided. I think a northern pine
        was present. At their wedding reception
people bet on how long their marriage would last.

Immediately after the ceremony, Gus's wife began
        to hound him with unreasonable demands:
"Get a job, you blowhard!" she bellowed. "Pay the bills!"
        "Pick up your underwear!" That sort of thing.

It lasted one day longer than the prenup: ten terror-filled
        years of drugs and booze and abuse on both sides.
There was, of course, a child who asked for none of this,
        but got it all.

Suicide

That angry leap from
       the overpass
the millisecond recognition
       of regret/relief
the gibbet constructed
       for those left behind
to hang themselves
       over and over
for the rest of their lives

The only way you had
       to kill them

Tough Luck

The ice was too thin
        no one could help
the swan its foot caught
        in ice on Walloon

All we could do is watch
        or not watch
as I chose to do

It was an eagle
        my neighbor said
that finished it off

A Mind of Winter

One must have a mind of winter.
Wallace Stevens

I have only the memory of the lake now,
of walking on its gelid surface, twenty below,
snowclouds envelop me, impart lessons
on my insignificance. The ice, two to four
feet deep in places, the dark slow world
underneath me, above, the white haze—
starlings, great blues, and the ghostly contrails
of sandhill cranes who have abandoned
the lake and its frosty beauty for the
California coast. Still, in my Psyche, I call
those birds and, like Echo, they answer.

Flashcuts

In the backseat of our old Oldsmobile
      two fresh pencils, unsharpened,

long, yellow.

I push one down my throat.
      I'm two years old.

I don't have words like
      emergency room, esophagus, choke.

Forty years later, a tense time in an English restaurant,
      while I work a fishbone out of my throat.

I climb on a high chair, maybe three years old,
      to grab my mother's "diet pills."

I chew them with glee,
      as if they were jellybeans.

My vocabulary doesn't include *stomach pump*,
      amphetamines, unconscious.

When language fails the body prevails —
      a lifelong fear of choking,

a heart still on a diet.

When there are no words,
      there's only psychic skin.

Back on the Farm

My father's death was easy enough,
or so it appeared. July 8, 1964,
a hot summer night in the
doldrums of Cheyenne.

I'd camped out on our couch
in the living room. His last
venture into my parents'
bedroom a passing blur—
the only time in my 14 years that
I didn't kiss him goodnight.

My mother's shrill voice
shattered the early-hour silence—
Ward! Ward! she cried.
His snores, loud and grating
staccato blasts—
only inhales.

At 4AM I straddled his body,
pounded on his chest like they
did on Ben Casey. His pinched
brow tight across his livid face:
he looked confused.

Sixty years now and I still
wonder what dream pierced
his psyche that last evening.

Was he back on the farm with
his brother Francis, sipping
warm milk from the pail
under their cow, or had he

fallen into their pond, his
tight muscular body caught
on something in the depths—
his breath, a temple of air,
held until that last
desperate gasp?

Longs Peak

Even in July we encountered chest high snow,
        corn snow they called it because of its
                nugget size.

In my early twenties I hiked up that mountain
        with my friend, John. I forgot to bring
                sunglasses—

a stupid rookie mistake. The white glare off
        granite and snow probably damaged
                my retinas forever.

Even through sun-bleached eyes the summit-
        view tasted like infinity, sounded like
                forever.

The jet that flew over us was, I thought, in reach.
        When we unpacked our lunch, a marmot
                joined us for his share.

The descent with John continued long after we
        came off the mountain. John was always
                a country whose language

I couldn't follow, whose terrain was foreign
        and unnavigable. Years later I discovered
                that his affection for me

camouflaged his desire for my wife whom he
        loved, but couldn't have. The rest of
                his story—

the three wives, the temper fits, the tragedies—
       is harder to tell than our hike, fifty years ago,
              through the blue blaze of a Colorado day.

Someplace Special

Since the phone rang
in the middle of the day
we felt no alarm. Judy
answered with a smile
that fell quickly to frown:
Someone had broken into
The Tree of Life Synagogue
on Shady and Wilkins
and opened fire on the congregation.

This was Pittsburgh, "someplace special,"
as the city slogan proclaimed.
What made it special to me,
a fallen Catholic and backslider Buddhist,
were the Jews walking the streets
of Squirrel Hill, Jews with kippot,
big bushy fur hats, prayer shawls
and fedoras, speaking Russian, Polish,
Hebrew, Yiddish, or the tangy
tongue of New York City.

Pittsburgh was someplace special
because I could leave shirts
at a laundry on Shady Avenue
and discuss the nature of light
in the Torah and in Heidegger
with the Jewish owner, or
attend a Passover Seder —
listen to arguments over Israel
and the true ancestry of Abraham,
or attend a lecture on Martin Buber
at the local Lubavitcher Shul.

But on that dreadful day,
October 27, 2018,
Pittsburgh, a city I loved,
was no longer someplace special,
but someplace shameful.
Eleven of its Jewish citizens
had been gunned down
because they wanted to pray.
Where might light be found
on such a dark day?
What would be its nature?

Nuremberg

After the painting by
Anselm Kieffer

The rows are straight. The Germans
are precise if nothing else.

The corn is gone, harvested,
warm inside the bellies of *das Volk*.

Dark and ugly furrows await winter, and what
a winter: Four years long, six million Jews long—

what happens when people deem one man
their savior, their thinker, relinquish

the unpleasant task of thinking for themselves. The
leader brands an entire people as the problem, as inhuman.

He becomes a tyrant of terror, a master of murder,
of extermination. Nothing is saved except the detritus

of idolatry, the ravaged fields of history, its factories
of destruction, smokestacks of shame.

Stupidity

For J.S.

Once it strikes
little can be done.
It's like a lightning bolt
that leaves everything
in its path scorched,
bleak, and stunned.

The guy in his MAGA cap
yells at my friend
that she's a scaremonger
for wearing a mask
while filling her car
with gas.

No matter that she had
a triple by-pass
only months in the past;
this ass knows best.
(Why do I need rhyme
to describe this crime?)

Factory Boss

After Henri Rouart in Front of His Factory,
a painting by Edgar Degas

He is the *pre* in post-industrial,
      the buttoned-up daddy of 'em all,
the tophatted, mustached, cigar smoker
      who paid his workers in turkeys
and Christmas ornaments.

Behind him his factory is shuttered—
      lonely as a Satie gymnopédie.
His workers port lunch pails,
      peasant shirts soiled from
poisonous toil in stacks of smoke.

This boss, the putrescence of production,
      caresses the creases of his pants
while his watch and fob dangle
      from the pockets of his waistcoat.
His gaze knife-edged, he opens
      the cover of his Elgin.
It's time, he thinks, for the second shift.

Legacy

Willy Loman would have wagged his head
in wonder. Does he even own a wallet?
Has he ever had to touch a dollar bill?
Does wealth exist, for him, outside
of articles in Forbes Magazine? How
did he convince Daryl or Dilbert,

Happy or Biff, that he was one of them?
Has he ever boiled water, made coffee,
fried an egg, scanned a want ad? Did
he ever gentle his hands through
his lover's hair and think,
this is where my soul lives?

For Freud, the sign of maturity was
the ability to delay gratification.
Did he ever stand in line, wait for
a paycheck, a bus, or put off
the simplest desire? Unfortunately,
for him, maturity wasn't for sale.

This man kept escaping *into* jail:
became an inmate of a prison called
Winning Is Everything where
Want Is Ought is written over the gate,
gold encrusts his convict's heart, and
the only fair way is on the golf course.

Superficial and Shallow, two phantoms,
board a jet, fly into ether. Contrails
produced by exhaust vaporize and fall,
eventually forgotten by all. He lost
the presidency, the House and Senate.
Finally, he made America great again.

After the 2020 Presidential Debates

Here's to the silence that stretches along the lake,
lets you hear a snowflake kiss its silver surface;
to what happens when you lift the needle
from the vinyl—that scratchless patch where
sound naps, where, as Miles told Trane,
you take the horn out of your mouth.

Salute what hides in the gap between your lips,
that quiet quotient of embrace, where we desire
only the best for each other, and for our country,
where orange becomes, once more, the hue
of pumpkin and autumn leaf, the space where
compassion, camouflaged, plots its escape

from slogans like Make America Great Again—
where those words plummet, headlong and forever,
into the murky depths of vitriol and venom, never
to be heard from again. Rise up, in this moment
of grace, dance a polonaise of decency, a ballet
of blessing. Behold the rest between notes, the
moment before the coda, the place of peace
and the untrammeled promise of calm.

To the Ruling Junta in Myanmar

In memory of U Sein Win, Chan Thai Swe,
Ma Myint Myint Zin, Ko Knet This, and
all the poets murdered by the junta in Myanmar

What do you beat
      when you beat a poet?
Ask Kerouac, Ginsberg, and Corso.
      We poets have always been beat,
whether beatific or cursed, we beat
      the cadence of existence,
its hope, despair, and dreams.

What do you kill,
      when you kill a poet?
A certain "I" enveloped in flesh,
      a boney bonnet that, once cracked,
releases a *mysterium tremendum* from its grip?

What do you accomplish
      when you eviscerate his corpse?
Don't you know that his guts, like his syllables,
      glide on thermals of unfettered breath?

What do you jail
      when you jail a poet?
A body, some bones,
      but you can't imprison liberty.
Freedom is the tablet
      upon which poets pen their lines.

What do you burn
       when you throw gasoline
on a poet and light him on fire?
       You can't incinerate inspiration.
Long after flames on flesh are extinguished,
       and governments rise and wither,
a poet's words burn their way through history.
       Mere death is hardly the matter.

IV

Miracles That Keep Me Going

For Judy

It's her sleek slacks on Mondays,
the way she waltzes into our porch-room,
even when in a wheelchair.

On Tuesdays it's her black and white
blouse that has always reminded me
of the strength of an orthodox
prayer shawl painted by Chagall.

How much I enjoy the careful way
she cuts into her eggs on Wednesdays—
how she portions a bit of yoke atop
a slice of bagel and eases it into
the mouth I've so often kissed.

On Thursdays it's her "Raindrops are
Falling On My Head" T-Shirt that causes
the corners of my mouth to rise.

Fridays bring blousy colors of blacks, blues,
orange, and turquoise with a splotchy scarf
to match that makes me think I'm
living with a Matisse painting.

It's her earrings that sparkle on Saturdays—
how they bounce and jangle against her
comely earlobes while she recites
a poem she's just written.

Then there are Sundays, our Sundays, where
her face, doe eyes, aquiline nose, and olive
skin turn our house into a temple of
her benevolent presence, a place
where the sacred blooms.

We All Know the End but Where Is the Middle?

*A question asked by Jim Harrison
in his novel,* Dalva.

It's in the backyard where the squirrels
have decimated our tulips but we smile,
shake our heads, in disgust, in delight:
we love both squirrels and tulips.

It's Judy's conviction that there's an
hallucinogen buried in a tulip's ovary,
because after eating a blossom one squirrel
dances wild across the yard, does

summersaults and backflips in midair.
I tell Judy that squirrel's been
crazy for years which makes me
wonder how long squirrels live.

The middle appears when the Forsythia
survives an April 1 blizzard—nature's
little April Fools' joke, and it's in
the magnolia's pink blossoms burned

umber in death by the freeze. It's
there when Judy scoots along in her
wheelchair, makes omelets even while
in pain, her eyes puddles of calm,

her voice the symphony of my life.
We are always in the middle, Jim,
until we reach the end.

Ace of Spades

After the painting by Chuck Olson

Even now night threatens to fell my chest.
A river that is my heart flows into an abyss,
a river you can't step into even once, and where
a brilliant crimson possibility meets the bloom
of the big bang. The planets, every photon,
quark, and black hole orbit wildly and collide.
The quasars are intense and stellar-hot. Fringe
space beckons, but fades finally into a filmy
cosmic sunset, takes a breath, opens a gap.
There's hope in this gamble called life where
that pulsing muscle chants, over and over,
Tomorrow, Tomorrow, Tomorrow.

The Prez

On Pandora I listen to
Lester Young's smokey sax
fly and twitter light
as a chickadee but
somehow deep as
a pale pool
of champagne left
by lovers who dance
alone, feet slow over
a living room carpet,
wrapped around each other
in a silence that only
Lester's sax could conjure.

This is what he could do—
play that bent brass
so sweetly,
so intimately,
that you could
mistake it for
the soundless embrace
of eternity.

Miles

Yours is the sound of smoke
    I love to inhale
        the sound of a humid
            summer night
            its cool breeze

Yours is the muffled sound
    of brass along my life
        of the hard streets
        of the stage floor

The sound of a dark copper chest

Your voice makes gravel tumble
    carefully, sparingly,
        through your horn

Each note selected
    to break our hearts,
        to break our backs
        to sift soul through
        our midnight world

Yours is the embouchure
    of struggle and triumph,
        of blue and prince
        of brew and bitch

Leitmotif

Was it Dvořák's Largo Theme I
first heard, or Sibelius' Finlandia,
or Tchaikovsky's First Piano Concerto?

I was so young, so fat, so troubled, but this music
took me to a place of melody and peace,
of harmony and happiness.

There I was, eight-years-old, in my basement,
standing atop the piano-shaped coffee table,
waving my baton at the monaural's spinning plate,

conducting the Cleveland Orchestra, pushing
Karl Kondrashin off his podium in Moscow,
making sure Van Cliburn kept to my tempo.

Arms sculpting the music, I gazed at placards
on the wood-paneled walls of my basement,
the pithy clichés hanging on them:

"When the going gets tough, the tough get going,"
"If you can't say anything nice, don't say anything at all,"
the drawing of the little man enclosed in a box—
"Someday I've just got to get organized,"

and photos of surfers in Malibu hanging ten,
or shooting the tube at Huntington Beach,
or sexy and tan beside their upright surfboards.

They were my audience. What did the tough
feel about the lilting second movement
of Tchaikovsky's concerto, the surfers think

as they rode waves to the Finnish National Anthem,
the cramped little man in the box as he listened to
the yearning in Dvořák's haunting theme?

Our Birch

Our birch is proud of her leaves,
doesn't worry about the inevitable fall;
proud as well of her umber-gray strength,
not against the cold and snow,
but with them: happy to be among
the living that thrive on gelid ground.

Our birch opens her limbs to talons
and beaks, accepts their feathered
gratitude with stately, upright grace,
yet bends in a breeze. She would have
been kind to Antigone, would have
granted her wish to bury her brother
no matter how much disgraced.

Her mouth is the rain,
her body the air we breathe.
She hugs tightly *terra sacra*
and never, ever, forgets
her roots in the earth.

Übermensch

Forty years ago, with smoke wafting
down our hallway and billowing
under the door and the fire alarm
blaring away, I had to get out fast.

My young wife was at work,
no animals to locate and save,
years away from our child's birth,
I grabbed what was, at the time,
my most valuable possession—something

I'd held dear since my first year at
the University of Wyoming where I sat
in Richard Howey's philosophy class,
sharpened my life, progressed it out of
the cave of conformity and complacency.
I grabbed my copy of *The Portable Nietzsche*
and fled our smoke-choked abode.

Outside, on the sunbleached sidewalk,
while helmeted Denver firemen wrapped
in their heavy rubber coats and boots,
stormed our building, I opened to *Zarathustra*
and read my favorite aphorism—a beatitude
Freddy wrote to Christians whom, he averred,

always slept well because they got God
to forgive their sins every night before bed:
"Blessed are the sleepy ones," he wrote,
for they shall soon drop off."

As it turned out, ours was a silly,
if smokey, dumpster fire, put out easily
by Denver's best. When my sweet wife
returned from her day's labor (I was still
struggling to obtain my BA), I told her
of the afternoon's excitement.

Had I wrapped arms around our wedding album?
she wanted to know. Had I carried it out of
our endangered building that day, rescued
our most cherished memories from the
inchoate flames? Her long dark hair,
moon-cool eyes, and hands whose fingers
moved over me like a Chopin etude,

instantly obliterated twenty years of Catholic
dogma about truth telling as well as my
adherence to Nietzsche's transvaluation
of all values. *Of course*, I replied. *I ran out
of our endangered home with our memories
held firmly in my hands, kept safe from
flames, hoses, water damage, and enemies:
foreign or domestic.*

That night I slept well. Dropped right off.

Something in Us Loves a Good Storm[5]

We turned onto Thumb Lake Road twenty-five years ago
in a blinding blizzard, a horizontal havoc of snow blowing
across our windshield. The windshield wipers couldn't
keep up with that northern Michigan blizzard.

To calm nerves and create distraction, Judy read
Harry Potter and the Philosopher's Stone aloud
to our sixteen-year-old son Ariel, and to me. Just
as she got to the part where there's an ominous knock

on the door during a ferocious storm where Harry
has been sequestered by the evil Dursleys, just at
that terrifying knock, our van went completely dark—
a starless, moonless, midnight encased our Honda.

Was Voldemort after us as well as Harry and Hagrid?
No—our harrowing experience was caused by hitting
a snowdrift that completely covered our van. This is it,
I thought. We'll be stuck here until they thaw out our

frozen corpses in the spring. I envisioned walking for miles
in below zero temperatures to find a kind farmer who would
let me use his phone to call for help. But then, as if Harry
had cast a Dissendium Spell, our conventional, non-four

wheel drive, gray, gasoline powered chariot carried us
through the storm and into Boyne City where we found
a restaurant, ordered a hot dinner, and renewed our wish
to find a place to live amid this arresting arctic beauty.

When our waitress, a young lady a little older than Ari,
asked for our drink orders, Ari ordered a coke and Judy
said she'd like a virgin bloody Mary. And when this
sweet maiden, festooned in the nascent bloom of femineity,

asked me what I wanted, I said I wanted a virgin. Our
waitress blushed, Judy frowned, and Ariel turned
the color of mortification. Having rescued my family
from the frozen fright of Northern Michigan and

having done my paternal duty of causing our son
to wonder what horrible curse Voldemort had
cast that made me become his father, I reclined
in my chair, smiled, and enjoyed the storm.

111

Our Old Place

This was well done, my bird.
William Shakespeare

I

At our old place on Walloon Lake
I looked out across brick-gray water
and let my mind sail along the silver surface.
Those daydreams, floated by a Rachmaninov
soundtrack, conjured a vague peace,
an imageless vision of calm.

II

My blue kayak, a two-seater, grasped
the lake's edge, waited patiently for me
to turn it over, stretch the waterproof skirt
from end to end, and place my tipsy corpus
into its welcoming shell.

III

Ariel, our son, climbed in one day. We
headed toward Mill Pond, about a mile
west of our place. Our paddle to Mill Pond
was a soft glide into a Monet at Giverny.
Once through the narrows, water lilies
carpeted the silt and sand of the pond.
On a whim we skimmed through the lacy
water to shore, pulled our kayak up to a
grassy ridge, and went exploring. About
five yards into densely packed woods,

we heard a mighty flapping. We stopped,
awed by invisible power. Seconds later,
a great brown avian arose only a few
feet from us. On that gray-sky day, Ari
and I had birthed to flight the winged
issue of a bald eagle.

IV

Back in our kayak, we turned toward home.
I looked at Ariel, my bird, sitting in the bow,
his paddle making broad sweeps against
the gunmetal sky. I felt his spirit fly
through my veins, magic my muscles,
nest in my heart.

Mugsi Doesn't Wear a Mask

But I do because of the pandemic.
        Mugsi doesn't because she's a dog,
a black standard poodle that
        we don't cut up to look like the freaks
owned by rich ladies in Manhattan.

On our walk we come across masked strangers
        who always appear menacing,
but who invariably wave because
        they are my neighbors and
we all like one another.

They remove their masks and I recognize them —
        a sheen of familiarity that brings relief.
It's always good to see what's behind a mask,
        even if the mask is an illusion of civility,
something that covers brutality and barbarism,
        even if what is unmasked is the bare bottom
of our culture, the butt end of racism,
        the guttural groan of fascism.

Mugsi wiggles her tushie while she walks,
        smells everything available,
is very intense, but always has time
        to wag her tail if we meet
a crossing guard who might
        have a treat for her.

Mugsi never holds a grudge even
   when it rains or snows too hard
for me to give her a walk.
   She always forgives me.
She loves to sit in my chair
   when I'm not in it,
and she knows exactly where she
   wants a scratch.

Shepherdess Bringing in Sheep

After the painting by Camille Pissarro

He died and, in despair, she took over the farm. She
put on a cheerful face when feeding the chickens,

coddled each seed when planting the corn, and cursed
the plow when her dress or apron caught iron.

Her sadness abated when calling the sheep who ran
to her bleating for her caring caress. These furry

beasts were her family now. Hope helped her open
the gate to greet their curious faces and not think

about the rickety fence she didn't have time to repair
or her life framed by the pallor of her lonely abode.

Architecture

After the painting by Paul Klee

Captured by the sullen night the building
speaks with sporadic light that leaks
from offices deserted for the nonce
as if devastated by blight. Empty
and enclosed by lonely coffers
steel and concrete towers wait
for dawn and business hours.

Ode to My Library

I

There you are, silent, stately,
the best minds, generous. You've
stood by me all these years, even
when I felt like saying goodbye.
There you were, paper and print,
patient and inviting.
I had to find out what message
our next quiet conversation
had in store for me—what
you wanted to pass on.

By the way, what do you do
at night when I'm not there?

II

I remember when I bought you,
Karamazov, dressed in your
Constant Garnet greatcoat. I
opened you on the sixth floor of
Orr Hall in 1968 for only $1.65.
In my room at the University
the brown plains of Laramie suddenly
communed with the windblown tundra
of nineteenth century Russia.

And you, Mr. Mayor, we met
in English class at St. Mary's
fifty-two years ago. I still savor
Hardy's gorgeous prose splayed

over every bump and weed
of those heath-hewn roads
and the memory of unrequited love
paved on every path in Casterbridge
and Cheyenne where I, a brokenhearted
teenager, first thumbed your pages.

And you, Papa, we're not supposed
to love you anymore, you who
in between booze bouts, bullfights,
and the blaze of war changed
American literature forever. You
taught me about grace, courage,
and the bounty of short sentences.
Thank you.

III

You've stuck with me, all of you,
from Aristophanes to Zola,
Brautigan to Waugh, Dickens to Roth.
And there you are, Walt Whitman,
"old grubber," as your posthumous
lover howled over time-ripples.
You kept the dooryard open,
guided my hand as I, an orderly
like you, emptied emesis basins,
dumped urinals during my own civil war
fifty years ago at Denver General Hospital.

119

IV

In the beginning you were two shelves
in Laramie, then you multiplied on my
bedside table in Denver. Your next home:
bricks and boards in Boulder until you took
your place, regal and proud, on store-bought
shelves in Pittsburgh. Now you occupy shelf
after shelf built into my attic study in the thirties.

I wonder, as I write, when I'll ease one of you
from your peaceful perch, open your musky pages,
and let you pour your wisdom into my thirsty heart.

Verdant

A word that Jack Kerouac loved to use in
On the Road—old Jack who hit the asphalt
with Neal Cassady in the late forties,

but didn't learn to drive until he was 34,
never obtained a driver's license, lived
with his mother, took up her occasional

antisemitism, nasty often to Ginsberg who
loved everything about Jack and who
chronically forgave him his faults. Jack,

after whom Ginsberg named The Jack Kerouac
School of Disembodied Poetics at Naropa University
maybe because he had to disembody Jack

to keep loving him. Meanwhile, Jack at home
with his mother, periodically brought a wife
to cohabit with sweet Gabrielle who

couldn't stand any of them. And Neal, who
drove electric while guzzling acid-laced
Kool-Aid, was loved by Allen into eternity.

Neal's spark plugs shorted out next to some
railroad tracks on a freezing night in Mexico
at age 41. Allen, who praised the beauty

of even Neal's ashes, outlived both him and Jack—
quietly slipped into an everlasting Buddha field
in his East Village apartment in 1997 at 71.

Only Allen, his queer shoulder pressed to
the wheel, achieved the verdant promise,
the poetic triumph, of Jack's road book.

The Truth About the Tomb

I could write a poem about the tomb,
how eternal rest, relieving at first,
quickly turns to boredom, something
I rarely felt in life.

My mother told me that, should
I find myself bored, I only have
to look in the mirror to find out why.
"Boredom is your own fault," she said.

"Not enough in life to interest you?
Why not? Poor you." Still, the tomb
would be a challenge. What's interesting
about death? It looks like death is dull—

dust still, graybrick-silent dull. Not
even a sneeze to break the monotony.
What about the heavenly hosts? God
on high? The pearly gates? Or, demons

of the dark, the fiery storm, the requisite
gnashing of teeth—all the biblical bilgewater?
I'll believe it when I see it. Until then
I'm sticking with the eternal blank,

the gap between notes, the primordial
nothing out of which something sprang
and back into which everything goes.
What's the remedy? Is there a solution?

Yes. I'm gonna get cremated, reduced
to a flakey pile of carbon particles. Parts
of me will find a place in the stomach
of a bass in Walloon Lake, or wash

ashore and become a heron's footprint,
or a morsel lodged between a deer's
molars—maybe transported by grub
and gobbled by a piliated woodpecker

who defecates and deposits slivers
of me on a golden heath to become
next year's corn crop, or trillium seed,
or the blazing blossom of a wood lily.

End Notes

[1] "The Flight from Womanhood," in Horney, Karen, *Feminine Psychology*, New York: Norton, 1923/1967, pp. 54-70.

[2] From *Whale Day*, by Billy Collins, Random House, 2020.

[3] The title is taken from the first line of David J. Thompson's poem, "Even on My Knees," in *Inside the Box 2020 Poetry and Art Collection Anthology*, Scars Publications.

[4] "The Girl from Ipanema Visits Detroit, 1964," in Diane Decillis, *When the Heart Needs a Stunt Double*, Wayne State University Press, 2021.

[5] From *The Windward Shore: A Winter on the Great Lakes*, by Jerry Dennis, University of Michigan Regional, 2012.

Acknowledgements

Across the Margin: "Our Birch"
Adelaide Literary Magazine: "French for Reading," "Myth Buster," "Failing Up"
Alien Buddha Press: "Grocery List"
Bluepepper: "Anniversary"
Burningwood Literary Journal: "Übermensch"
California Quarterly: "Hot Poems to Go"
Cultural Weekly: "Dyslexia," "Writer's Block"
Edison Literary Review: "Leitmotif"
The Ekphrastic Review: "Shepherdess Bringing in Sheep," "Architecture"
Gasconade Review: "Enlightenment," "Flashcuts," "Mugsi Doesn't Wear a Mask," "We All Know the End but Where Is the Middle?"
Harbinger Asylum: Enlightenment
Home Planet News: "Full Body Exam," "Trepanning," "Hotboxing," "Back on the Farm," "Miracles That Keep Me Going," "Cowbell"
The Honest Ulsterman Magazine: "The Cremains Tour"
Ibbetson Street 49: "The Fly in the Ointment"
Impspired Magazine: "Coin Collection," "Late Lament," "Penis Envy," "Attention," "To the Ruling Junta in Myanmar," "Night of the Iguana"
Jerry Jazz Musician: "The Girl from Ipanema, Washakie Center, the University of Wyoming, 1969"
Jerry Jazz Musician, A Collection of Poems Devoted to Miles Davis: "Miles"
Literary Heist: "Suicide"
The Mountain: An Anthology of Poetry and Microfiction in Celebration of Mountains: "Longs Peak"
Muddy River Poetry Review: "The Prez"
Nixes Mate Review: "Switching Lanes"
Oddball Magazine: "After the 2020 Presidential Debates"
Open: Journal of Arts and Letters: "Nuremberg"
Pangolin Review: "Elephant Loaf"
The Paterson Literary Review: "The Old Days," "Something in Us Loves a Good Storm"
Piker Press: "Failing Up"

Poetry Life and Times: "Tough Luck," "Factory Boss"
The Poetry Superhighway: "Silent Night"
*The Poetry Superhighway 23rd Annual Yom HaShoah (Holocaust Remembrance
       Day) Poetry Issue*: "Someplace Special"
The Ravens Perch: "A Mind of Winter"
Red Fern Review: "Loneliness"
The Silent World in Her Vase: "The Truth About the Tomb," "Ode to My Library"
Spectrum: "I Don't Bother Much with God"
Unlikely Stories Mark V: "The Truth About Alaskan Air"
Vox Populi: "Stupidity," "Out of the Closet"

"Something in Us Loves a Good Storm" was awarded third place in the 2021
Allen Ginsberg Poetry Contest sponsored by *The Patterson Literary Review*

The author would like to thank the following for their support of his work:
Julie Albright, Jenny Ashburn, Valerie Bacharach, Jay Carson, Steve Cawte,
Dar Charlebois, Jim Daniels, Diane Shipley DeCillis, Susan and Greg Deny,
Don Drife, Hedy Sabbagh Habra, Jodi Haven, Maxine Heller, David
Hornibrook, Jim Hutt, Nadia Ibrashi, Jason Irwin, Lori Jareo, Sheila Kelly,
Diane Kerr, Larry Kohler, M.L. and Pam Liebler, Caroline Maun, Tayloe
McDonald, Gary Metras, Lindsey Manthei O'Conner, Sand Polanski, Bill
Richards, Judith Robinson, Mother Seraphima, Artie Solomon, Elizabeth
Solsburg, Keith Taylor, Paul Kareem Tayyar, Cody Walker, Kevin Walzer, and
my muse, life companion, and first reader, Judy Brice.

Made in the USA
Monee, IL
22 July 2023

39569742R00080